A TASTE
OF THE
HOCKING
HILLS

A TASTE OF THE HOCKING HILLS

Matt Rapposelli

Ohio University Press

Athens, Ohio

Ohio University Press, Athens, Ohio 45701
ohioswallow.com
© 2018 by Ohio University Press
All rights reserved

Printed in the United States of America
Ohio University Press books are printed on acid-free paper ∞ ™

28 27 26 25 24 23 22 21 20 19 18   5 4 3 2 1

Unless otherwise indicated, all photos are by Kelly Sabaiduc/Loyal Sun Photography.

Photos on pages xviii, 1, 2, 22–23, 48–49, 66, 89, and 92–93
are used by courtesy of the Hocking Hills Tourism Association.

The photo on page xxii is used by courtesy of the Hocking Hills
Tourism Association. Photo by Eric Hoffman.

The photo on page 87 is used by courtesy of Ricky S. Huard.

Library of Congress Cataloging-in-Publication Data

Names: Rapposelli, Matt, author.
Title: A taste of the Hocking Hills / Matt Rapposelli.
Description: Athens, Ohio : Ohio University Press, [2018]
Identifiers: LCCN 2018019599| ISBN 9780821423226 (hc : alk. paper) | ISBN
   9780821446362 (pdf)
Subjects: LCSH: Seasonal cooking--Ohio--Hocking Hills. | Cooking (Natural
   foods)--Ohio--Hocking Hills. | Hocking Hills (Ohio)--Pictorial works. |
   LCGFT: Cookbooks.
Classification: LCC TX907.3.O32 H637 2018 | DDC 641.5/6409771835--dc23
LC record available at https://lccn.loc.gov/2018019599

This book is dedicated to my mom, Nelda Rapposelli.

Whether you knew it at the time or not, your endless hospitality and the way you approached cooking and food paved the path I've followed. That copy of *The Joy of Cooking* that you sent with me as I left home is well worn, and your notes inside will be forever treasured. I can never thank you enough for everything. You did well . . .

contents

introduction

My arrival in the Hocking Hills has brought a culinary and outdoor journey full circle. Like many chefs, I grew up in a home that centered around a love of food, as well as the business of food. Both my Italian father and my grandfather were involved in the food business. When I was a young boy, Saturdays meant going to one of the grocers my father did business with and getting to eat whatever specialties they were making that day. The sights, smells, tastes, and characters of those trips have never left my memory. Combine that with a mother who approached cooking not as a chore, but as a subtle passion. Dinner was almost always at the dinner table in the dining room, and everybody was always welcome. Food was real and not to be confused with any pseudo ingredients; she had always claimed that margarine was not something people should eat and, during the craze of "butter is bad," that they would one day come to realize the error of their ways. She firmly believed that if it was natural and had been eaten for all of time, it was not to be messed with. I never knew how much this affected me until I struck out on my own.

Growing up, I loved being outdoors. As my wings grew, I took any opportunity to go hiking, backpacking, canoeing—anything that got me out

into the beauty of nature. I embraced the changing of the seasons. I loved not only the striking visual changes each season brought, but also all of the seasonal smells. When I was old enough to drive, I would tell my folks that I'd go to the later Mass at church on my own. What they didn't know was that my church was one of the local parks and that my worship was celebrating the natural beauty around me as I hiked. I decided my calling was to become a park naturalist, somebody who was outdoors and interacting with people. I did just that, eventually working for the National Park Service in Washington State. It was a dream job in a dream location . . .

You can't deny genetics. I was meant to make a living with food. It has the most overwhelming draw on me. The people, the process, the universal language of food. No words are needed to bring vastly different people together when food is the bond. I left the Park Service to pursue all things food, going to culinary school in Vermont and trying to find my niche. I worked my way around all different types of foods in many different places, but the beauty of my mother's southeastern Ohio kept calling. I settled in and embraced all the area has to offer, a stunning wild landscape as well as a vibrant food community.

The Hocking Hills area is where I've been able to unite my two greatest joys. When an opportunity came to start a restaurant within one of the most spectacular parks the state has to offer, as well as to work alongside many friends from my park days, I couldn't resist the lure. The first restaurant my partner and I started was at Lake Hope State Park, quickly followed by taking over the operation at Hocking Hills State Park as well. Running a restaurant adjacent to the most heavily visited state park meant unpredictable extremes in both the number of diners each day and the wildly varied requests. Not only did we have thousands of day-trippers coming to the area, but there are hundreds of unique private cabins and lodging options in the Hocking Hills. Fortunately, those looking to be

"away from it all" still appreciate well-prepared, scratch-made food. This combination was too appealing—getting to cook local specialties for appreciative guests in a stunning natural setting that ebbs and flows with the seasons. During the peak of the tourist season, when local produce is plentiful, it takes all we have to feed so many. My favorite time of the year in the Hocking Hills is winter. The pace slows, we get to spend more time with our guests, and the locals come to catch up with one another. Combine that with a magical snowfall that blankets the dense hemlocks and a hearty meal next to the fire. It really doesn't get much better.

I hope that this book will be a warm reminder of your experiences in this unique region or a draw for those who have not yet visited.

part 1

SPRING

Spring in the Hocking Hills is the fascinating yearly rebirth of countless natural wonders. For many people it's their favorite season in this area. Each year I'm entranced by the almost imperceptible visual changes that unfold before our eyes. I compare the experience to watching a black-and-white photograph morph into ultra-high-definition 3-D colorful splendor. The variety of wildflowers brings admirers from all over to catch a glimpse of the numerous elusive species we are fortunate enough to have. The many waterfalls are at their peak, drawing photographers to their cool mist.

The sights, the sounds, the smells . . . and the food! The four big spring highlights for all the food lovers in this region are the morel mushrooms, the ramps, the asparagus, and the abundant wild turkeys. You will start hearing folks at the lodge asking, "Have you seen any morels yet?" The same conversations are heard at the local gas station and shared on social media. The hunt grants bragging rights for "How many did you find today?" and is marked by great secrecy as to where the best hunting grounds are!

This time of year makes it so easy to incorporate the local bounty into our dishes and provides the gateway to what's to come.

Asparagus with Morels

The combination of local morel mushrooms and fresh asparagus is the flavor of spring in this area. Italy and France have their truffles; we have morels. There are so many possibilities for these gorgeous Alice in Wonderland–looking fungi, but I prefer keeping it simple and letting their flavor and texture shine next to fresh asparagus. If you are not fortunate enough to find morels growing nearby in the wild or for sale at your local farm market, morels have recently become commercially available in many places, with Oregon being a big producer. While the price may seem steep, it doesn't take a large quantity of them to make an excellent dish.

Serves 4

- 2 Tbsp butter
- 2 Tbsp extra-virgin olive oil
- ½ lb fresh asparagus, sliced into ¼-inch-thick slices on a sharp bias
- 1 lb fresh morels, halved from top to bottom and cleaned
- 1 tsp minced fresh garlic
- Salt and pepper to taste

1. Heat butter and oil in a heavy-bottomed skillet over high heat until they are shimmering.

2. Add asparagus and toss until it turns bright green.

3. Add morels and cook until the liquid is released and is mostly gone.

4. Remove from the heat, toss in the garlic, and keep tossing for 1 minute.

5. Season with salt and pepper to taste.

Broccolini with Balsamic Vinegar and Lemon

Although broccolini used to be an item found mainly at ethnic grocers, it is becoming far more common in local markets lately. A number of local growers have added it to their offerings in recent years. It is a great change from broccoli, and the texture is a perfect complement to a wide variety of dishes. The addition of this quickly prepared vegetable to your meals will really refresh your taste buds!

Serves 2

   1 Tbsp olive oil
   ½ lb broccolini, broccoli, or broccoli rabe
   ¼ cup water
   ¼ tsp minced fresh garlic
   2 Tbsp balsamic vinegar
   ½ tsp lemon zest, finely grated
     Salt and pepper to taste

1. Heat oil in a cast-iron pan or a wok over high heat until it starts to shimmer, just before it starts to smoke.

2. Toss in broccolini and stir constantly for 1 minute.

3. Add water, cover, and steam until water is evaporated.

4. Add garlic, toss for 30 seconds.

5. Add balsamic vinegar, lemon zest, salt, and pepper. Toss and serve.

Orange Tomato Basil Soup

This is one of the simplest dishes you will encounter. It always brings rave reviews and requests for the recipe. At first glance the combination seems a bit odd, but it produces the perfect mingling of sweet, savory, and satisfying.

Makes about 4 bowls or 7 cups

- 3 Tbsp extra-virgin olive oil
- 2 large carrots, peeled and chopped
- 1 medium yellow onion, chopped
- 2 tsp minced fresh garlic
- 1 28-oz can diced tomatoes
- 1 bunch fresh basil leaves or 1 Tbsp dried basil
- ¼ tsp baking soda
- 1 cup orange juice (more or less to taste)
- Salt and pepper

1. Put the olive oil in a 4-quart pot over medium heat until the oil is hot.

2. Add the carrots and the onions and cook, stirring frequently, until the carrots are soft, about 15 minutes.

3. Add the garlic and cook 1 minute more.

4. Add the tomatoes and cook until they start to simmer.

5. Add the basil and transfer the ingredients to a food processor or blender. If using a blender, remember to leave the lid cracked a bit and cover it with a kitchen towel to allow room for the hot liquid to expand. If you fully close the blender top, soup will blow all over when you turn the machine on!

6. Run the processor or blender until the mixture is smooth and uniform.

7. Pour the mixture back into the pot on low heat and stir in the baking soda. This step removes any acidity from the tomatoes without having to add sugar.

8. Add the orange juice and salt and pepper to taste.

Cave Side Salad

This is a colorful and flavorful entrée-worthy salad. It is a nod to the original lodge's proximity to Old Man's Cave, located just below the dining room's windows. It can be made in any size you choose, from one serving to enough for a gathering. Just adjust the ingredients to your liking.

Make ahead: Grill, smoke, or sauté ½ to 1 lb of boneless chicken breast or thigh meat, making sure to season the meat with salt and pepper before cooking. Slice and allow to cool.

> 1 bowl of greens of your choice (We use a combination of a spring mix and baby spinach.)
> Oil-packed sun-dried tomatoes, drained and chopped
> Toasted almonds, chopped
> Dried cranberries, or any combination of dried fruit of your choice
> Shredded carrots
> Cucumber, diced
> Red onion, thinly sliced
> Chèvre-style goat cheese
> Champagne Vinaigrette (recipe follows)

1. Place as much of your greens blend in a bowl as you would like. The rest is a matter of your tastes.

2. Top the salad with the ingredients in any amounts that suit you. When using the sun-dried tomatoes, remember they have a robust flavor, so be mindful not to add too much until you taste the mix. You can always add more. Keep in mind the colors and textures as you place them atop the greens. Alternate colors and textures so the salad has an appealing look.

3. Drizzle enough of the champagne vinaigrette to lightly coat the salad.

Champagne Vinaigrette

Champagne vinegar is made from the same grapes as the famous sparkling wine. What sets this vinegar apart from others is a very clean, crisp flavor. It is a bit more mellow than white wine vinegar, and it goes quite well with fruit and herb vinaigrettes.

  3 Tbsp Champagne vinegar
  1 Tbsp honey
  1 Tbsp red onion, finely chopped
  1 clove garlic, finely minced
  2 tsp Dijon mustard
  ½ tsp kosher salt
  ¼ tsp freshly ground black pepper
  ¼ cup extra-virgin olive oil

1. Whisk together vinegar, honey, onion, garlic, Dijon mustard, kosher salt, and freshly ground pepper in a small bowl.

2. Gradually whisk in olive oil until blended.

Pan-Seared Chicken with Balsamic Rosemary Tomatoes

A very quick and simple recipe that gives the impression you have spent a substantial period of time in the kitchen! Just a few ingredients that really complement one another make for a very flavorful dish.

Serves 4

  1 Tbsp extra-virgin olive oil
  4 boneless chicken breasts, seasoned with salt and pepper
  1 strip bacon, chopped
  ¼ cup red onion, diced
  ¼ tsp minced fresh garlic
  4 cups Roma tomatoes, diced
  ¼ tsp fresh rosemary, minced
  ½ tsp balsamic vinegar
     Salt and pepper to taste

1. Heat a sauté pan over medium-high heat and add olive oil. When hot, sear the chicken breasts on both sides until the internal temperature is 160°F and each side is a golden caramelized color. Make sure not to crowd the pan or else the temperature will drop and the chicken will not develop the color. Remove chicken to a plate to rest.

2. Reduce the heat to medium, add bacon, and cook until just brown. Add onion and garlic and cook until translucent. Add the tomatoes and rosemary and heat just until tomatoes are warm. You want them to retain their body and not be cooked to a mushy consistency.

3. Finish with balsamic vinegar and season to taste.

4. Top seared breasts with tomatoes and serve.

part 2
SUMMER

Once summer is upon us, we are in full swing!

The park is buzzing with activity daily. The hike down into the caves offers a welcome break from the humid warmth above. Families are having experiences that will translate into lifelong memories and generational traditions—coming back year after year to the same cabin their grandparents had brought them to and meeting at the lodge to share meals and stories of their explorations and finds of the day. We host guests from around the globe, all in awe of the unexpected beauty they have discovered in this corner of our state. It is the perfect opportunity to highlight the local bounty we have at our fingertips to transform into flavorful fare: blueberries from Chad the "Blueberry Guy" for our cobblers; the most spectacular lambsquarters, basil, and rhubarb I have ever seen in my life from Dr. Rudy's gardens; and never-ending squash and tomatoes from the Baileys, just to name a few.

Frittata with Roma Tomatoes, Fresh Basil, and Manchego

Fresh basil and Roma tomatoes are my ultimate combination. I look forward to this time of year for this pairing alone. While there are so many varieties of tomatoes to choose from during the summer months, I love the Roma for its ability to hold its texture for fast, hot cooking and its minimal seeds, letting the basil highlight the tomatoes in this dish.

Serves 2–3

- 2 Tbsp extra-virgin olive oil
- 6 large eggs, beaten
    Pinch Italian seasoning
    Salt and pepper to taste
- 2 ripe Roma tomatoes, diced
- ¼ tsp minced fresh garlic
- ½ cup shredded Manchego cheese
- 8 large leaves fresh basil, stacked and rolled together lengthwise, as if you were rolling a cigarette, and sliced into the thinnest strips you can with a very sharp knife

1. Preheat oven to 400°.

2. Place a cast-iron pan over medium heat and add olive oil.

3. Mix eggs, Italian seasoning, salt, and pepper.

4. When oil is very hot, add tomatoes and stir for 30 seconds. Add garlic, toss, and then pour in egg mixture.

5. Sprinkle shredded cheese over egg mixture and place pan in oven.

6. Bake until frittata is puffy and set in the center, about 10 minutes.

7. Remove from oven, sprinkle sliced basil over top, and serve.

Bruschetta with Roma Tomato and Basil Topping

This is a quick and fresh bruschetta topping that highlights the simplicity of the best of tomato season. Salting the tomatoes pulls out excess liquid and concentrates the tomato essence, giving the bruschetta a wonderful texture and great flavor.

Topping

- 5 Roma tomatoes
- 2 Tbsp kosher salt
- 12 fresh basil leaves
- 2 Tbsp diced red onion
- 1 tsp minced fresh garlic
- 2 tsp extra-virgin olive oil
- 2 Tbsp shaved Parmigiano cheese
- Black pepper
- Crisp Breads for Bruschetta (recipe follows)

1. Dice the Roma tomatoes and place them in a wire mesh sieve. Add the kosher salt and toss together. Let them drain in the sieve over the sink for at least 15–20 minutes.

2. Stack the basil leaves and roll them together lengthwise, as if you were rolling a cigarette. Slice the rolled leaves into the thinnest strips you can with a very sharp knife.

3. After your tomatoes have drained for the appropriate time, very briefly rinse them under running water to remove excess salt, and let them drain again for a few minutes.

4. Put the tomatoes in a bowl, add the remaining ingredients, and toss together.

5. Adjust the pepper and salt if necessary and serve.

This not only makes great bruschetta, but it's also excellent as a sandwich topping or addition to pasta dishes.

Crisp Breads for Bruschetta

Baguettes are a perfect size for these appetizers, but any type of crusty, hearty bread will work.

> 1 loaf bread of choice
> Extra-virgin olive oil
> Butter, melted
> Salt

1. Preheat oven to 350°.

2. Cut the bread into ¼-inch slices and into the desired shape.

3. Combine extra-virgin olive oil and melted butter, making just enough to coat the bread.

4. Brush both sides of the bread with the olive oil and butter mixture.

5. Salt very lightly.

6. Place the bread on a cookie sheet pan and place in the 350° oven until just toasted and slightly golden.

7. When cooled, top with the tomato and basil mixture.

Fried Catfish

Because of the close proximity of many rivers, catfish is really popular around this region. I was a latecomer to the catfish bandwagon. So often it had a silty or "muddy" flavor that was off-putting to me. That all changed when I discovered that you can, in fact, find catfish with a sweet, clean flavor. This recipe accents the flavor of the catfish without overwhelming it with a heavy, greasy crust. I try to find American farm-raised catfish whenever possible. Given the unknowns in the origins of imported fish and the widespread contamination of wild waters, it seems to be one of the best choices. Using American farm-raised catfish also reduces the chances of getting that "muddy" flavor so often associated with wild fish or imports.

Serves 4

> 4 8–10 oz American farm-raised catfish filets, each cut in half lengthwise leaving 2 narrower, thick pieces
> 2 cups buttermilk
> 1 Tbsp Tabasco or your favorite hot sauce
> 2 cups catfish breading (recipe follows)
>   Oil for frying

At least 8 hours ahead:

1. Mix buttermilk and hot sauce together in a bowl.

2. Add catfish filets and make sure they are covered by the buttermilk. Place in the refrigerator for at least 8 hours or best overnight.

Immediately before serving:

3. Heat enough oil to cover the fish filets in a heavy-bottomed pot or deep fryer, to 350°. Cast-iron pans work best for this.

4. Remove catfish from buttermilk, shaking off any excess liquid.

5. Coat each filet with the breading mix and lightly press the mix onto the fish, making sure every surface is covered.

6. Lay as many filets into the hot oil as will fit without crowding the pan.

7. Cook for about a minute and a half per side for a total of about 3 minutes, until they are golden brown.

8. Drain on paper towels and serve with tartar sauce (recipe follows) or cocktail sauce.

Catfish Breading

Makes 3¼ cups

    1 cup all-purpose flour
    1 cup corn meal
    1 cup masa harina (Mexican tortilla flour)
  1½ tsp Cajun seasoning
  1½ tsp granulated garlic
  1½ tsp Old Bay seasoning
  ¾ tsp black pepper
  ¾ tsp kosher salt
  ¼ tsp cayenne pepper

1. Combine all ingredients in a mixing bowl and blend well.

2. Store in an airtight container in a cool, dark place.

Notes: Masa harina is a specialty corn flour that is used to make fresh tortillas. The corn is dried, milled, and treated with a lime-and-water process that gives it a unique flavor and texture. It is available at many standard grocers and any Hispanic market.

Granulated garlic is different from garlic powder. It is a bit coarser, and because of this it holds up to higher-heat cooking without losing flavor or becoming bitter. It can be found at most grocers or any spice shop such as Penzey's in Columbus and other cities as well as online.

Tartar Sauce

Scratch-made tartar sauce tastes so much better than store-bought. It also costs much less and is very quick to throw together. It will keep for quite a while in the refrigerator.

Makes 1½ cups

    1 cup Hellmann's mayonnaise (or your favorite brand)
  ¼ cup dill relish
    1 Tbsp white onion, minced
    1 Tbsp malt vinegar
      Dash white pepper

Combine all the ingredients in a bowl and whisk together.

The sauce can be used immediately, but gets better if it can sit overnight in the refrigerator.

Pico de Gallo

This is a quick, fresh salsa that will change the way you use fresh tomatoes. It is the harbinger of tomato season for me. Salting the tomatoes pulls out excess liquid and concentrates the flavor, giving your pico a heartier consistency and great taste. Soaking the red onions in vinegar water removes that hot burn sometimes associated with raw onion. We call it deflamming.

Makes 1½–2 cups

5	Roma tomatoes
2	Tbsp kosher salt
1	Tbsp red wine vinegar
¼	cup water
2	Tbsp minced red onion
1	tsp minced fresh garlic
1	small jalapeno pepper, diced small
2	tsp extra-virgin olive oil
½	fresh lime, squeezed
2	Tbsp chopped fresh cilantro
	Black pepper

1. Dice the Roma tomatoes and place them in a wire-mesh sieve. Add the kosher salt and toss together. Let them drain in the sieve over the sink for at least 15–20 minutes.

2. Add the vinegar to the water in a small dish and add the red onion. Let soak about 5 minutes.

3. After your tomatoes have drained for the appropriate time, very briefly rinse them under running water to remove excess salt, pour the onions and vinegar water over them in the sieve, and let everything drain again for a few minutes.

4. Put the tomato and onions in a bowl, add the remaining ingredients, and toss together.

5. Adjust the pepper and salt if necessary and serve.

Grilled Vegetables

This is one of our most-requested recipes at the lodge. People are always surprised at how easy the grilled vegetables are to prepare. It goes back to simple combinations that highlight the flavors of each ingredient. The colors are as vibrant as the flavors. This is a dish that is great for gatherings, as it can be done ahead and still taste great, as well as be served at room temperature if the need arises.

Makes 4 servings

> 1 medium zucchini
>
> 1 medium yellow squash
>
> 8 large, whole button or cremini mushrooms
>
> 4 Roma tomatoes, cut in half lengthwise
>
> 4 green onions, roots trimmed
>
> ¼ cup extra-virgin olive oil
>
> 1 Tbsp minced fresh garlic
>
> 2 tsp Italian seasoning
>
> 1 tsp kosher salt
>
> 1 tsp coarse ground pepper

1. Cut the tip and stem off the zucchini and the yellow squash. Then slice each squash lengthwise into ¼-inch slabs. Slicing them this way keeps them from vanishing into a fiery inferno between your grill grates.

2. Place all of the remaining vegetables, the zucchini, and the squash in a large bowl or shallow roasting pan. You want enough room to be able to work the marinade into all the vegetables.

3. Add the oil, garlic, Italian seasoning, kosher salt, and pepper.

4. With your hands, lovingly massage the seasonings and oil into all of the vegetables, making sure they are evenly coated.

5. Cook the vegetables on a really hot grill, preferably over charcoal, until they are tender and have a nice grilled look to them. Just a heads-up: the green onions will take only a minute or so.

Note: This is not a recipe that requires the vegetables to marinate for any length of time. If you want to marinate the vegetables ahead of time, leave the salt out of the marinade and mix it in just before grilling. If you add it too long before you grill, it will make the squash watery and give it a less firm texture.

Barbeque Brisket

Barbeque brisket is probably one of the most intimidating cuts of meat to cook properly. This is one that can't be rushed; there are no shortcuts to moist and tender brisket bliss. Time and temperature control are the key factors for this to turn out perfectly. A good-quality smoker and a high-quality, instant-read thermometer make your chances of success much greater. The succulent brisket is also great in Brisket and Blue Salad (page 76) and Meaty Mac (page 80).

The first thing you will need to do is find what is called a packer brisket. This is the whole brisket with both pieces of the muscle and all of the fat intact. These are sometimes stocked in your local grocers and most always are available at the club stores. These are large, usually around 9 lb or more. A brisket has two parts, one called the flat and one called the point, separated by a fat layer. The brisket typically stocked at the grocery is a trimmed piece of the flat (think of the pieces you see used for corned beef), which alone does not work well for long, slow smoking.

Once you find a packer brisket, you will want to coat it liberally with the Barbeque Spice Rub over all of the meat's surface, top, bottom, sides. Don't be shy. Don't succumb to the urge to trim any fat off of the meat at this point! You will want it all to lovingly baste the meat while it is smoking. You also will want to make sure your brisket is cold right from the cooler when you put it in the smoker. That will help the smoke penetrate the meat, giving you the most flavor.

I can't cover here all of the different setups for smoking that are available these days, but the basics are the same no matter what equipment you have. The one smoker/grill purchase I have made over the course of the last thirty years that I can't recommend enough is called the Big Green Egg. I have owned and used dozens of grills and smokers, and this one has no comparisons. The key to barbeque/smoking success is the ability to consistently maintain set temperatures for long periods during the cooking process. For brisket, you want to cook/smoke the meat at 225° for anywhere from 9 to 15 hours. This is the mystery of the brisket. The only determination of when it is ready is when the internal temperature hits 180°. There is no rushing the process, and every brisket cooks a little differently. Patience and vigilance will give you that ethereal brisket you are dreaming of!

Barbeque Spice Rub

This is our basic barbeque seasoning that we use on our brisket and pork. It makes a great base to start from, and then you can add or alter spices to your tastes.

- 1 cup kosher salt
- ¾ cup brown sugar
- ⅓ cup granulated sugar
- ½ cup coarsely ground black pepper
- ¼ cup granulated garlic (See note on page 32.)
- 2 Tbsp granulated onion
- ¾ cup dark chili powder
- ⅓ cup ground cumin
- 2 tsp cayenne pepper

1. Place all of the ingredients in a bowl and mix until thoroughly blended.
2. Store in an airtight container.

Batter-Style Cobbler

We do two styles of cobblers at the lodge. One is the traditional batter style, which is very quick to put together and works with many types of fruits. The other style we offer is a streusel-topped variety bursting with whole mixed berries (see page 62). The batter style gives you a very nice cake-like texture intertwined with your fruit filling. The streusel-topped one gives you a very nice layer of thickened mixed berries punctuated by the crisp accent of the streusel.

2 cups fresh or frozen blueberries (Peaches, raspberries, or strawberries work well too.)

1 Tbsp lemon juice

¼ tsp orange zest

1 tsp vanilla extract

¼ tsp cinnamon

¾ cup sugar

½ cup (1 stick) butter

¾ cup sugar

1 cup all-purpose flour

2 tsp baking powder

½ teaspoon salt

¾ cup milk

1 egg, slightly beaten

1. Preheat oven to 350°.

2. In a saucepan, combine the berries, lemon juice, orange zest, vanilla extract, cinnamon, and first ¾ cup sugar. Bring to a boil; remove from heat and set aside.

3. Place the butter in an 11 x 7-inch baking dish and place in the 350° oven until the butter is melted.

4. In a small bowl, combine the remaining sugar with the flour, baking powder, salt, milk, and egg.

5. Pour the batter over the melted butter in the baking dish. Do not stir.

6. Spoon reserved berry mixture over batter. Do not stir.

7. Bake at 350° for 40–45 minutes or until golden brown.

8. Serve at room temperature with whipped cream or ice cream.

part 3

FALL

The arrival of fall in the Hocking Hills is for

many the most-anticipated season. The temperatures start to change, with crisp sunny days and cool clear nights. The stars burst from the coal-black autumn night sky, and in the daytime, the changing foliage offers a color palette unmatched anywhere in the world. There is a brief and much-appreciated slowing down from the summer frenzy as people return to their jobs and school begins, but it is short lived. All of the lodging has been booked a year in advance in anticipation of scoring a stay during the peak of the colors. The roads are busy with "Leaf Peepers" on the hunt for the most picturesque vantage point and a stop at the local apple orchard. A visit to try all of the varieties of apples you will never see in your local grocer and to drink one of their apple cider slushies is an experience like no other.

All of this means the lodge will be a beehive of activity, playing host to many day-trippers for lunch and cabin guests in the evenings. Our local produce starts to change as well. Gone are the perfect and flavorful tomatoes, as well as the intoxicating smell of basil. In their places we start to see chanterelles and oyster mushrooms, kale and cabbage, and many varieties of squash and pumpkins. We are, after all, located just down the way from the nation's largest pumpkin festival.

Buttermilk Pancakes

Waking up to the smell of freshly made pancakes is a defining moment of trip to the Hills. This is a very often requested recipe from the lodge. No commercial mix can come close to the flavor and texture of this recipe. You can make a mix of the dry ingredients and keep it in the freezer to have a ready supply on hand.

Makes about 25 medium-sized pancakes

    4 cups all-purpose flour
    ½ cup sugar
    1 Tbsp plus 2¼ tsp baking powder
    1 tsp baking soda
    1 tsp salt
    4 cups buttermilk
    4 large eggs
    1 stick plus 2 Tbsp melted butter

1. Whisk all of the dry ingredients together.

2. Add the eggs and buttermilk and whisk the batter until it just comes together. It should look a bit dry yet.

3. Add melted butter and blend until it is evenly moistened.

4. Cook in a very lightly buttered pan over medium heat until you see small bubbles across the surface, then flip and cook until the center sets. There is no need to add any more butter after the first pancake; this will help you get that beautiful golden color across the surface.

You can add any ingredients you like to these. After you pour the batter into the pan, sprinkle berries, granola, chocolate chips, bacon, or sausage across the top and continue to cook as usual.

Chicken Hominy Soup

This is a very flavorful and bold soup, perfect for crisp fall evenings. I've always thought hominy is an underutilized ingredient. It has a great meaty texture as well as a bold corn flavor that works well in many dishes. If you are not familiar with hominy, it is corn kernels soaked in a lye or lime solution that softens the hull and the germ. It is then washed away, leaving the swollen kernels that now have a starch-like texture. You can find canned hominy in most grocery stores as well as in any Hispanic market.

Makes about 4 bowls or 7 cups

- 3 Tbsp extra-virgin olive oil
- 1 cup chopped onion
- ½ cup chopped celery
- ½ cup thinly sliced carrot
- 1 Tbsp minced fresh garlic
- 2 tsp dark chili powder
- 2 raw boneless chicken breast halves or boneless chicken thighs, cut into thin strips
- 1 quart chicken stock
- 1 cup whole canned hominy
- ½ cup pulverized corn tortilla chips (Pulse in a blender or food processor.)
- 1 lime, juiced
- ¼ cup chopped cilantro
  Salt and pepper

1. Place a 4-quart or larger pot on medium heat. Add olive oil and onion, celery, carrot, garlic, and chili powder. Cook until celery is tender.

2. Add chicken strips, stir, and then add stock and hominy and bring to a low boil.

3. Add pulverized tortilla chips, stir, and cook 3 minutes longer.

4. Add lime juice, cilantro, and salt and pepper to taste.

Wild Mushroom Soup

We are fortunate to be in an area rich in seasonal wild mushrooms: morels, chanterelles, oyster, chicken of the woods, and puffballs, to name a few of the most popular. Many of these varieties are available through commercial sources as well, and make great-tasting and unique soups. If none of these varieties is available, you can use a mix of commonly available mushrooms from your local grocer. Pick up some of every variety you can find—button, cremini, portabella, oyster, or enoki—to use in your soups.

Makes about 4 bowls or 7 cups

> 3 Tbsp butter
> 2 Tbsp extra-virgin olive oil
> 4 cups sliced fresh mushrooms (Mix as many types as you are able to find.)
> ½ cup chopped red onion
> 2 tsp minced fresh garlic
> ½ cup dry white wine (Use a wine you would actually drink, not a cheap cooking wine.)
> ¼ tsp minced fresh lemon zest
> 1 tsp chopped fresh thyme (½ tsp dry)
> 2 cups heavy cream
> 2 cups half-and-half
> Salt and pepper

1. Place a 4-quart pot over high heat, add the butter and olive oil, and heat until the oil shimmers.

2. Add the mushrooms and onion. Stirring often, cook until the mushroom liquid is almost gone.

3. Add the garlic and cook for 30 seconds more.

4. Add the wine and cook until the liquid becomes syrupy.

5. Add the lemon zest, thyme, cream, and half-and-half and reduce the heat to medium. Cook until the soup just starts to simmer. Adjust seasoning with salt and pepper to taste and serve.

Pumpkin, Corn, and Bacon Fritters with Smoked-Pepper Aioli

These are fast to put together, and the basic recipe is quite versatile. No pumpkin? Use any orange squash or sweet potato. Want bolder flavor? Use a really sharp cheddar or a local goat milk cheese. As long as you use the first 8 ingredients, you can add whatever sounds good at the moment. The possibilities are endless, and the results will still be quite addictive!

Makes 18–25 fritters

1	cup all-purpose flour
1	Tbsp sugar
1	tsp baking powder
½	tsp salt
1	egg, beaten
½	cup milk
1	Tbsp buttermilk
1	Tbsp bacon fat or butter
1½	cups finely shredded fresh pumpkin
1½	cups whole corn kernels, fresh or frozen
¾	cup shredded Monterey Jack cheese
4	oz cooked bacon, chopped
	Oil for frying

1. Mix flour, sugar, baking powder, and salt in a mixing bowl.

2. In another bowl combine egg, milk, buttermilk, and bacon fat or butter and blend.

3. Fold into the wet mixture the pumpkin, corn, cheese, and bacon.

4. Add the wet mix to the dry and fold together.

5. Heat enough oil in a pan to completely cover fritters, at least 3 inches deep, to 350°.

6. Use a tablespoon to drop batter in small batches into oil and cook about 3 minutes until golden and cooked through. Do not overcrowd the pan, as you want to have enough room to turn the fritters.

Serve with the aioli.

Smoked-Pepper Aioli

¼ cup mayonnaise
½ tsp smoked paprika or chipotle pepper powder

Mix mayonnaise and pepper powder together and set aside.

Roasted Pumpkin with Red Onions, Sage, and a Balsamic Drizzle

Pumpkin is huge in this region, both literally and figuratively. One just shy of 2,000 pounds was on display at the local annual pumpkin festival. Many varieties with specific purposes are available. This recipe showcases pumpkin in a tasty and attractive way that is worlds away from the canned stuff.

1   small fresh sugar pumpkin (or butternut squash), peeled, seeded, and cut into uniform ¼-inch-thick slices

1   small red onion, peeled and sliced top to bottom into ¼-inch strips

    Extra-virgin olive oil

10 fresh, whole sage leaves (or to taste)

    Salt and pepper

    Balsamic vinegar

1. Preheat oven to 400°.

2. Toss pumpkin and onion with enough olive oil to coat, season with salt and pepper to taste, and add as much sage as you would like.

3. Spread pumpkin mixture in a single layer on a baking pan and roast in the 400° oven until pumpkin is tender (about 30 minutes), turning every 10 minutes.

4. Remove from oven, place in a serving dish, and drizzle with balsamic vinegar to taste.

Streusel-Topped Berry Cobbler

This recipe has been a staple for the lodge since our first day open. Its popularity has been surprising, and the requests for the recipe, abundant. The beauty of this version is the ease of preparation. You can make the streusel topping ahead of time, even keeping batches on hand in the refrigerator, and it is easily expanded to match any size pan you choose to bake in. Putting it together takes minutes, and the results are excellent.

Filling

- 5 cups fresh or frozen mixed berries (blueberries, strawberries, raspberries, blackberries, cherries)
- 1 cup sugar
- 5 Tbsp cornstarch or tapioca flour

1. Combine all of the ingredients in a mixing bowl and toss together, blending well.
2. Pour into a greased 8 x 8-inch pan.

Streusel topping

- 1 cup all-purpose flour
- ½ cup brown sugar, packed
- ½ cup (1 stick) unsalted butter, cubed
- 1 tsp cinnamon

1. Preheat oven to 350°.
2. Combine all the streusel ingredients in a food processor and pulse until crumbly, or cut the ingredients together in a bowl with a fork.
3. Top the filling with the streusel and bake at 350° for 45–60 minutes. The cobbler is done when the filling is bubbling in the center of the pan.
4. Let cool and serve with whipped cream or ice cream.

part 4

WINTER

The leaves are gone, the campgrounds are

empty, and an overall serenity has returned to the area. Winter is my favorite season in the Hocking Hills. The most magical and anticipated moment during this season is to be in the lodge next to a warming fire, looking out on falling snow as it is caught by the boughs of the massive hemlocks above the caves. Our guests change during the winter. What just a few short weeks ago was a cacophony of visitors from around the world has been replaced by the locals reemerging from their hectic schedules of taking care of their own guests. It's an annual reunion of sorts, a celebration. We made it through another season, and it's time to reconnect. Not just as a business transaction, but as friends. The visitors to the area during the winter are a hardier lot, adventurous and determined. We use this time to regroup. It's also the time we can get really creative with special requests for meals. We always do what we can to make special orders, but winter gives us the luxury of time. Our guests know this, and the requests keep us on our toes. Our choice of locally available foods narrows considerably. We have processed and stored all we could during the peak of the season—berries, rhubarb, and other fruits and vegetables, all waiting to make a guest appearance and bring a flashback of summer to a blustery evening.

Hocking Hills Granola

This is a fairly time-consuming recipe—a perfect indoor activity for a cold winter day. The house will be filled with the most inviting scents as the granola bakes, and your efforts will be rewarded many times over as you enjoy it for days to come. It can be stored in an airtight container for weeks and is the perfect addition to many other recipes. We sprinkle some of this on our buttermilk pancakes as we cook them. They're always a hit.

Makes 17 cups

- ½ lb coarsely chopped almonds
- ½ lb chopped pecans
- ½ lb whole pecans
- ½ lb chopped hazelnuts
- ½ lb raw pumpkin seeds
- 1½ lb oats
- 1½ Tbsp cinnamon
- 1 tsp nutmeg
- 1 tsp salt
- ¾ cup packed light or dark brown sugar
- ¾ cup canola oil
- 1¼ cups honey
- ¼ cup vanilla extract
- ¼ lb dried cranberries
- ½ lb golden raisins
- ¼ lb dried cherries, coarsely chopped
- 7 oz shredded sweetened coconut, lightly toasted

1. Preheat oven to 225°.

2. Mix the first 10 dry ingredients (almonds through brown sugar) together in a bowl large enough to add the rest of the ingredients.

3. Combine all of the wet ingredients in a bowl and blend well. Reserve ¼ cup of the liquid.

4. In a bowl toss the cranberries, raisins, and cherries with the reserved ¼ cup liquid.

5. Add the remaining liquid to the oat mixture and blend well.

6. Spread oat mixture onto 2 large sheet pans and bake at 225° for 1½ hours, stirring every 15 minutes.

7. When you take the finished oat mixture from the oven, place it in your large bowl, add the fruits and coconut, and combine.

8. After it cools, the granola can be stored tightly sealed in a cool, dry place for up to 2 months.

Note: This also makes a great addition to pancakes. After you pour your batter down, sprinkle the granola mix onto the batter and continue to cook as usual.

Clam Chowder

This recipe is one I brought back to this area from my time in New England. It's straightforward and quite simple, but the results are all that a proper clam chowder should be—hearty and flavorful. It freezes quite well should you want to make extra for meals down the road.

Makes about 4 bowls or 7 cups

- 2 Tbsp olive oil
- 4 strips raw bacon, chopped
- ¼ cup celery, chopped
- ½ cup onion, diced
- 1 cup potatoes, cut into ¼-inch cubes
- 1 tsp minced fresh garlic
- 4 Tbsp flour
- 1 cup clam juice
- 2 cups milk
- 1 cup heavy cream
- 2 cups chopped canned clams with reserved juice
- 1 tsp fresh chopped thyme or ½ tsp dried thyme

1. Place a large pot over medium heat, add olive oil and the bacon, and cook until the bacon just starts to get some color.

2. Add the celery, onion, and potatoes and cook until the celery starts to soften.

3. Add the garlic, cook for 1 minute, and then add the flour and incorporate thoroughly.

4. Add the clam juice, milk, and heavy cream and stir thoroughly while bringing the soup to a gentle boil for 3 minutes.

5. Add the thyme and stir.

6. Stir in the clams with reserved juice, bring back to a simmer and serve.

Buttermilk Biscuits

We are in southeast Ohio. This is the northern line of biscuit fanaticism. If you try to serve a substandard biscuit, you will hear about it. Mostly in a polite "my mother's biscuits were a little different" kind of way. You learn pretty quickly how people want their biscuits, and scratch-made ones are the only option. The recipe couldn't be any simpler. But often therein lies the rub, as they say. It's all about technique when it comes to the difference between an "okay" biscuit and a "wow, I want another!" Do not be drawn into overworking the dough. A light touch and keeping things cold will help you achieve success. As with anything, practice. Make a few batches back to back. You will see what works well and what doesn't. Once you have the touch, your biscuits will evoke a longing for another.

Makes 1½–2 dozen biscuits

- 2 cups all-purpose flour, plus more as needed
- 2 tsp baking powder
- 1 tsp salt
- ½ tsp baking soda
- 8 Tbsp (1 stick) cold unsalted butter, cut into ½-inch pieces
- 1 cup cold buttermilk

1. Arrange a rack in the middle of the oven and preheat to 425°. Grease a baking sheet or line it with parchment paper.

2. Whisk the flour, baking powder, salt, and baking soda together in a large bowl.

3. Add the butter pieces and toss to just coat them in the flour mixture.

4. Working quickly and using a pastry blender or 2 knives so as not to soften the butter, cut the butter into the dry ingredients until it's in pea-sized pieces.

5. Pour in the buttermilk and stir just until a moist, shaggy dough comes together.

6. Generously dust a work surface with flour. Scrape the dough out onto the surface and dust the top with more flour. Using floured hands, gently pat the dough into a 1-inch-thick rectangle. Do not be tempted to overwork the dough—leave it slightly loose and shaggy.

7. Using a chef's knife, cut the dough into 2-inch squares.

8. Transfer the biscuits to the prepared baking sheet, spacing them at least 1 inch apart.

9. Bake until the biscuits have risen and are golden brown on top, about 15 to 16 minutes.

Brisket and Blue Salad

This is the most popular salad at the lodge. It is a great combination of salty, smoky, meaty, and savory. This is one of those dishes that is hearty and yet will also transport you back to the warmth of summer around the smoker. This is best made as an individual salad for the visual appeal, but you can cut all of the ingredients into bite-size pieces and toss everything in a bowl for a quick option for feeding a group.

Makes one entrée-sized salad

In a large salad or pasta bowl, add the following ingredients in the order they are listed. Serve with blue cheese dressing (recipe follows) and warm sweet potato rolls (recipe on page 86).

- 2 cups chopped romaine lettuce
- 2 Tbsp shredded carrots, placed at the 12 o'clock position on the lettuce in the salad bowl
- 4 ¼-inch-thick slices of Roma tomatoes layered atop the lettuce at the 6 o'clock position
- 6 ¼-inch-thick slices of a cucumber cut in half lengthwise and placed in the 3 o'clock position
- 6 thin slices of red onion placed in the 9 o'clock position
- 2 ¼-inch-thick slices of warm smoked brisket (recipe on page 38) laid across the center of the salad, keeping some of the vegetables underneath visible
- 3 Tbsp crumbled blue cheese sprinkled over the brisket

Blue Cheese Dressing

½ cup blue cheese crumbles (first quantity)

½ cup sour cream

½ cup mayonnaise

¼ cup buttermilk

2 Tbsp minced red onion

1 clove garlic, minced

½ tsp freshly ground black pepper

½ cup blue cheese crumbles (second quantity)

1. Combine all but the second ½ cup of blue cheese crumbles in a food processor and blend well.

2. Transfer to a mixing bowl and fold in the second ½ cup of blue cheese crumbles.

3. Adjust consistency with additional buttermilk if you choose.

Meaty Mac

This is one of our signature dishes—simple, but it hits all the right flavor and texture notes. It is very easy to prepare for a family meal as well as large events.

Makes 8 generous portions

- 1 lb elbow macaroni or penne cooked al dente in salted water and drained thoroughly
- ½ cup (1 stick) butter
- ½ cup flour
- 4 cups milk
- ½ tsp salt
- ¼ tsp black pepper
- ¼ tsp granulated garlic
- 1 lb shredded sharp cheddar cheese (or any combination of cheeses you would like)
- 1 lb American cheese, diced (Velveeta works best)
- 1 lb cubed smoked brisket (recipe on page 38)
- 1½ cups shredded sharp cheddar for topping

1. In a saucepan, melt the butter over medium heat and then stir in the flour. Stir and cook until the flour is evenly incorporated.

2. Add the milk and the spices, stirring constantly until the mixture starts to thicken, about 8 minutes.

3. Stir in the 1 lb shredded and 1 lb diced cheeses and stir until they are melted into the sauce and it is smooth and creamy.

4. Combine the sauce with the pasta and the brisket in a 9 x 13-inch baking pan, top with the 1½ cup shredded cheese, and place under a broiler until the cheese is melted and bubbly.

Noodles

One of the defining foods of the Hocking Hills region, and this part of Appalachia, is noodles served over mashed potatoes. It was one of the combinations that most stood out to me when I arrived many years ago. I couldn't quite understand serving a starch on top of another starch. In my travels, when asked about the foods of our area, this was the one I most talked about. It didn't take me long to embrace the beauty of this comforting combination. When the noodles are scratch-made and cooked in a rich chicken stock peppered with pieces of chicken meat, the flour from the noodles thickens the stock and you end up with one of the simplest and most satisfying dishes you can imagine. The noodles are as easy as can be to make, and with so few ingredients you will notice a difference when you use the best eggs you have access to, preferably ones that are local and from chickens that have been fed well. The noodles can be cooked in salted water for plain buttered noodles or in beef stock for beef and noodles or added and cooked in soups as well. The turmeric gives the noodles a more vibrant yellow color to contrast nicely with the mashed potatoes.

Serves 8

> 2 cups all-purpose flour
>
> 2 whole eggs
>
> 1 tsp salt
>
> ½ tsp turmeric (optional)
>
> 2 quarts chicken stock
>
> 1 raw boneless chicken breast, sliced thin

1. Place the flour in a mixing bowl with the salt.

2. Add the eggs and blend together until the mixture becomes a smooth ball. Can be done by hand or with a stand mixer.

3. Wrap the dough in plastic wrap and let sit in the refrigerator for half an hour.

4. Divide the dough into 2 pieces.

5. Roll each piece out on a floured surface, getting the dough as thin as you can. The noodles will thicken when they are cooked, so you don't want to roll them too thick.

6. Lightly flour the top of the dough and roll it up from one edge to the other.

7. With a sharp chef's knife, cut the dough into ¼-inch strips or any width you choose.

8. Unroll the strips on your cutting board and liberally flour the cut noodles, taking care to separate them.

9. In a large pot, bring the stock to a simmer with the chicken breast strips and add the noodles, taking care to stir as you add them to keep them from clumping. Let the noodles simmer for about 15–20 minutes until they are tender.

10. Remove from the stove and ladle the noodles with some broth over mashed potatoes to serve.

Mashed Potatoes

   3 lb Yukon Gold potatoes or a similar variety

  ½ cup (1 stick) butter—real butter (not margarine, *real* butter)

  1 cup heavy cream

  ½ cup half-and-half

     Salt and pepper to taste

1. Peel the potatoes and cut into 1-inch chunks.

2. Place potatoes in a large pot of cold water, enough to generously cover them.

3. Bring potatoes to a boil and let cook until just tender.

4. In a small saucepan or microwave-safe bowl, combine the butter, cream, and half-and-half and heat through until the butter is melted.

5. Once potatoes are tender, drain them and place them back in the pot, off the heat. This will help dry the potatoes a bit and give them a fluffier texture.

6. With a potato masher or heavy whisk, mash the potatoes until they are uniform.

7. Add the cream and butter mixture and mash until they are light and fluffy.

8. Add salt and pepper to taste.

Sweet Potato Rolls

It's rare to go to a restaurant these days that actually makes its own rolls. People may think it is just too time consuming and requires a specific skill set that is not easily found any longer. These rolls are a foundation of our restaurant. People are often too intimidated to bake breads, but these are pretty straightforward and forgiving. It's a basic, classic recipe, but we use sweet potatoes in ours in place of white potatoes. It gives the rolls a gorgeous color and a depth of flavor you don't get with white potatoes. Nothing is better on a cold winter night than the smell of these rolls coming out of the oven, just before you tear one apart and spread it with butter.

Makes 18 large rolls

2	large eggs
¼	cup sugar
2	tsp salt
6	Tbsp softened butter
1	cup cooked sweet potato, mashed
2½	tsp dry yeast
¾	cup milk
4	cups all-purpose flour
	Melted butter for brushing rolls

1. Preheat oven to 350°.

2. Mix all of the ingredients together in a mixer or by hand and knead until a smooth, soft dough develops. You may have to add a bit more flour.

3. Place the dough in a lightly greased bowl and cover with plastic wrap. Put in a warm place to rise until the dough has doubled in size, about an hour to an hour and a half.

4. Deflate the dough and divide it into 18 equal-size pieces.

5. Round each piece into a smooth ball and place on a greased sheet pan. You can place the balls side by side if you would like pull-apart-style rolls or space them about 2 inches apart if you would like individual rounds.

6. Cover with plastic wrap that has been sprayed with cooking spray.

7. Let them rise until they have doubled in size and bake them in a 350° oven for about 20 minutes until they are golden brown.

8. Brush them with melted butter after you take them from the oven.

Note: These also freeze quite well, should you want to make a batch for the future.

part 5

SPRING AGAIN

The last of the ice has melted, and the water
is cascading over the falls, providing a sonic backdrop for the spring peepers to showcase their vocals. The black-and-white landscape is slowly trans-
forming back into the rich, colorful quilt that will soon draw thousands of
nature lovers back to the area. Just like the morels and the asparagus, we
emerge from our temporary isolation to greet another season head on.

Sautéed Lambsquarters

Lambsquarters (also spelled lamb's quarters) is a really common plant that grows naturally in many areas of the United States and Canada and is considered a weed by some. It is also incredibly delicious and a favorite vegetable for the late spring and early summer. It has a texture like a meaty spinach and an asparagus-like flavor. Most everyone who tries it becomes a fan. My favorite way to prepare it is a quick sauté in a blazing-hot skillet. It gives it a slight smoked hint that goes with most anything and is quick and painless to prepare. Like fresh spinach, lambsquarters cooks down quite a bit. It is a great addition to pasta dishes as well, giving them a unique twist.

Serves 2

   1 Tbsp grapeseed oil, or an oil of your choice that can withstand high-temperature cooking
   ½ lb fresh-picked lambsquarters, washed, excess water removed
   ½ tsp minced fresh garlic
   1 Tbsp extra-virgin olive oil
   Salt and pepper to taste

1. Place a large, heavy-bottomed skillet over high heat and add the grapeseed oil. Heat until the oil just starts to smoke.

2. Immediately add the lambsquarters and continuously toss until the leaves wilt and become a deep, dark green.

3. Remove the pan from the heat, add the garlic, and toss until it is evenly incorporated.

4. Add the extra-virgin olive oil, season with salt and pepper, and serve.

conclusion

Having the opportunity to live and work in the Hocking Hills has been a gift. I love the people, the landscape, and the foods. So many people are passionate about food in this area—a passion that comes from an inherent appreciation for honest, real foods and the sharing of meals based on that passion. No pretense, no show, just the simplicity of the joy of real food.

Bringing all three of these together—the people, the landscape, and the foods—brings me my joy. To play a small part in someone's experience when they visit and dine with us, possibly becoming a part of their tradition along the way, is the greatest reward. I hope your experiences in the Hocking Hills have ignited a passion that will continue to burn for many more generations.

Now go ahead and pass that plate along . . .

acknowledgments

First, I must acknowledge photographer Kelly Sabaiduc for her contributions to this book. From our meeting at the Hocking Hills State Park to working together at the lodge, we've followed a circuitous route to this end.

I also thank the entire staff at Ohio University Press, in particular editors Gillian Berchowitz and Rick Huard, for their hard work in bringing this project to fruition. This book would not have been possible without their efforts.

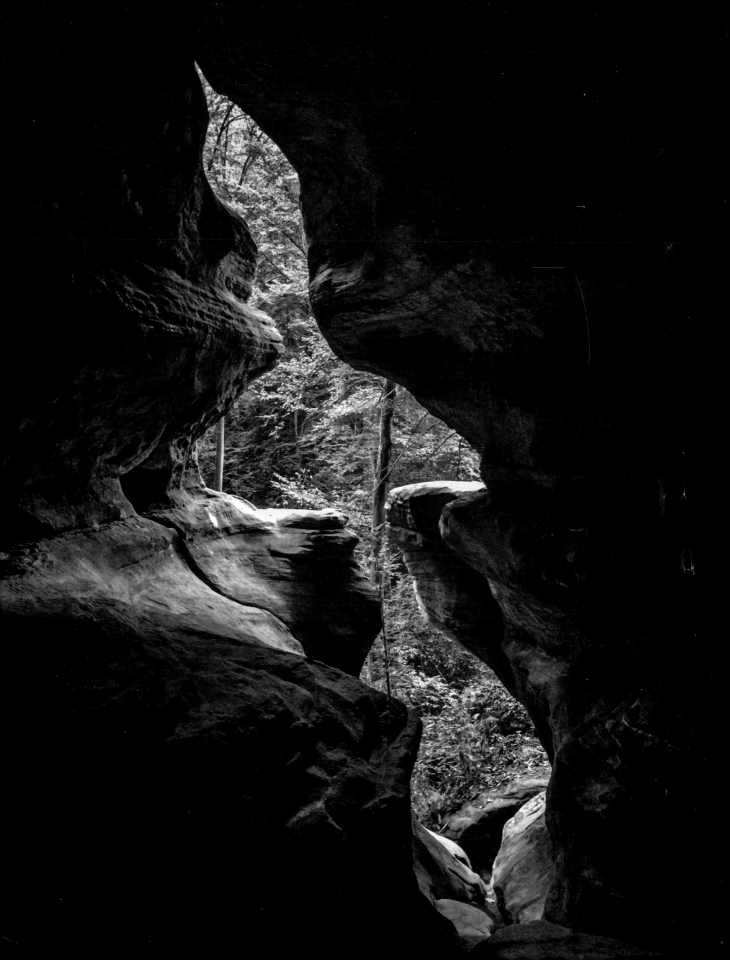